Fact Finders

Great Inventions

THE RADIO

by Gayle Worland

Consultant:
Jonathan Winter
President, American Museum of Radio
Bellingham, Washington

Capstone press

Mankato, Minnesota

Fact Finders is published by Capstone Press,
151 Good Counsel Drive, P.O. Box 669, Mankato, Minnesota 56002.
www.capstonepress.com

Copyright © 2004 by Capstone Press. All rights reserved.
No part of this publication may be reproduced in whole or in part, or stored in a retrieval
system, or transmitted in any form or by any means, electronic, mechanical, photocopying,
recording, or otherwise, without written permission of the publisher.
For information regarding permission, write to Capstone Press,
151 Good Counsel Drive, P.O. Box 669, Dept. R, Mankato, Minnesota 56002.
Printed in the United States of America

Library of Congress Cataloging-in-Publication Data
Worland, Gayle.
    The radio / Gayle Worland.
        p. cm. — (Fact finders. Great inventions)
    Includes bibliographical references (p. 31) and index.
    Contents: The power of the radio—Before the radio—Inventors—How a radio works—
The radio becomes popular—The golden age and today.
    ISBN 0-7368-2217-8 (hardcover)
    ISBN 0-7368-4542-9 (paperback)
    1. Radio—Juvenile literature. [1. Radio.] I. Title. II. Series.
TK6550.7 .W62 2004
621.384—dc21   2002156503

Editorial Credits
Roberta Schmidt, editor; Juliette Peters, series designer and illustrator; Alta Schaffer,
    photo researcher; Eric Kudalis, product planning editor

Photo Credits
Austin Schmidt, 14–15, 17, 18
Classic PIO Partners, cover, 26 (all), 27 (left)
Corbis/Bettmann, 5, 11, 19, 22, 25
Corel, 1, 27 (right)
Hulton/Archive Photos by Getty Images, 6–7, 8, 9, 12 (both), 13, 20–21, 23
Image Library, 27 (middle)

1 2 3 4 5 6 08 07 06 05 04 03

Table of Contents

Chapter 1

The Power of the Radio

Aliens from Mars have landed in the state of New Jersey!

Millions of people heard that message on the radio on October 30, 1938. The story was not true. It was part of a radio program by the actor Orson Welles. The story came from a book called *The War of the Worlds*.

"The War of the Worlds" program sounded so real that people got scared. Thousands of people called the police and asked what to do. Many people ran from their homes, taking food, clothes, and other supplies with them.

Many people helped with "The War of the Worlds" radio program.

Some people were so upset that they had to go to the hospital. The people's actions showed the power of the radio.

Chapter 2

Before the Radio

In the late 1800s, people used a telegraph or telephone to send news messages. The invention of the radio changed the way people heard news.

The telegraph sent messages over wires in Morse code. An operator changed letters into dots and dashes. Another operator received the messages. That operator changed the dots and dashes back into words.

Telegraph operators sent and received messages in Morse code.

Morse Code	
A	. −
B	− . . .
C	− . − .
1	. − − − −
2	. . − − −
3	. . . − −

The telegraph let people send messages over long distances, but it had some problems. People had to go to telegraph offices to send messages. Most people did not know Morse code. They had to ask the operator to send and read their messages.

The invention of the telephone in 1876 made sending messages easier. The telephone let people talk to each other directly. But like the telegraph, the telephone needed wires to send messages. Messages could only travel between places connected by wires.

With the telephone, people could talk to each other directly.

Before the radio, sailors waved flags to send messages to shore and to other ships.

Ships at sea could not use telegraphs or telephones. They had to flash lights or wave flags to send messages to each other.

The radio did not need wires for its messages. It sent messages through the air. For this reason, some people called the radio "the wireless."

Chapter 3

Inventors

The radio was not invented by one person. The idea for the radio grew out of the work of many people.

Early Discoveries

In 1864, James Clerk Maxwell explained how electricity and magnetism work together. He said they make waves that people cannot see. The waves move at the speed of light. They travel 186,282 miles (299,792 kilometers) per second. These waves are called electromagnetic waves. Radio waves are one type of electromagnetic wave.

James Clerk Maxwell was a Scottish physicist.

Heinrich Hertz was a young German scientist.

In 1888, Heinrich Hertz showed that Maxwell's electromagnetic waves were real. Hertz was the first person to send radio waves over a short distance.

After Hertz, Nikola Tesla worked with these waves. In the early 1890s, Tesla built a wireless system. It sent and received radio waves from 30 feet (9 meters) away. Tesla believed that one day everyone could send and receive wireless messages.

Nikola Tesla was a Serbian-American inventor.

Father of the Radio

Guglielmo Marconi is sometimes called the father of the radio. Marconi was from Italy. He was the first person to send radio signals over a long distance.

In 1901, Marconi sent a Morse code signal by radio from England to Canada. The message traveled more than 2,000 miles (3,200 kilometers).

Marconi showed his "wireless telegraph" to the King of Italy. He also showed it to the Queen of England and many other important people. He and his radio became famous.

Guglielmo Marconi was an Italian physicist and inventor.

Marconi did not like school until he started to learn about chemistry and physics. He loved to study electricity.

Chapter 4

How a Radio Works

A radio receives messages sent on electromagnetic waves. Radio stations use transmitters to send these waves. The waves carry messages of news, music, and sports. These messages are called broadcasts.

A radio station turns sound waves into broadcasts through several steps. First, a person at the radio station talks into a microphone. The microphone changes the voice into electric signals.

Radios in people's homes
receive broadcasts.

Microphone

Transmitter

Radio waves carry broadcasts from a radio station to a personal radio.

These signals become part of the program signal. Next, the program signal is added to a carrier wave. The carrier wave then is sent through the station's transmitter. Finally, the transmitter sends the wave into the air.

A radio in a person's home or car receives the carrier wave. The radio separates the program signal from the carrier wave.

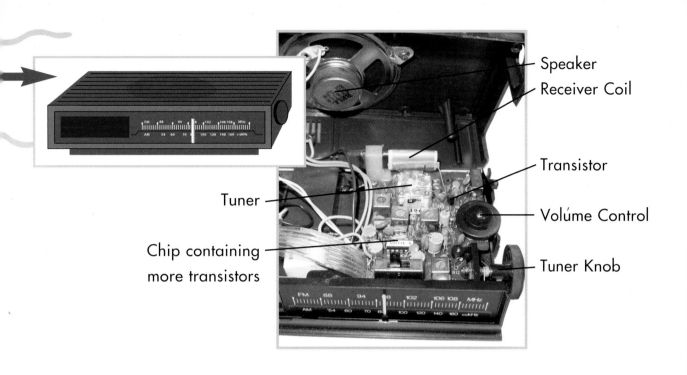

Speaker

Receiver Coil

Transistor

Tuner

Volume Control

Chip containing
more transistors

Tuner Knob

Then, the radio turns the signal into words and music. A radio listener can then hear the words spoken into the radio station's microphone.

Frequency

Each radio station has its own frequency for sending signals.

The unit of frequency is named after Heinrich Hertz. The hertz (Hz) is equal to one cycle per second.

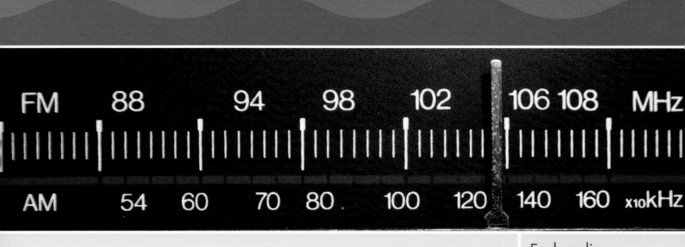

FM 88   94   98   102   106 108   MHz
AM   54   60   70 80   100   120   140   160   x10kHz

Each radio
station has its
own frequency
for broadcasting.

Radio frequency is the number of
complete radio waves in one second.
People "tune in" to a radio station by
setting their radio to receive a certain
frequency. Amplitude Modulation (AM)
radios receive waves with frequencies
between 535,000 and 1,700,000 hertz.
Frequency Modulation (FM) radios
use waves with frequencies between
88,000,000 and 108,000,000 hertz.

Old and New

The earliest radios were powered by large batteries. After 1927, radios were powered by the electricity in people's homes.

Early radios were different from radios today. They were much bigger. They used large glass containers called vacuum tubes.

The invention of the transistor in 1948 changed radios forever. The transistor worked like the vacuum tubes, but it was much smaller. Radios could be made small enough to fit in a person's hand.

A transistor (left) is smaller than a vacuum tube (right).

Chapter 5

The Radio Becomes Popular

In the early 1900s, few people thought the radio was important. Most radios were found only on ships. Sailors talked to people on other ships and on shore. Then, in 1909, two ships ran into each other in the Atlantic Ocean. One ship used the radio to call for help. Most of the passengers were saved. After that rescue, people understood how the radio could be useful.

The first official radio station was KDKA in Pittsburgh, Pennsylvania. It went on the air November 2, 1920.

KDKA broadcast the 1920 U.S. presidential election. Radio listeners knew who won the election before the newspapers arrived the next day.

People made sounds for radio programs with bells, fake guns, and other noise makers.

On December 24, 1906, Reginald Fessenden made radio's first broadcast. It was Christmas Eve, so he played holiday songs and read from the Bible.

That day was the election day for the 29th U.S. president. KDKA broadcast the election. People who owned radios heard that Warren G. Harding was the new president. People without radios did not know until they read the newspaper the next day.

After 1920, hundreds of radio stations began to broadcast. But during the early years, radio stations used the same frequency. Broadcasts often got mixed up with other stations' programs. Radio listeners could not understand the messages.

In 1927, the United States formed the Federal Radio Commission (FRC). Today, this group is called the Federal Communications Commission (FCC). It makes sure that each station in an area has its own frequency.

The BBC

In 1928, the British Broadcasting Corporation (BBC) began to broadcast news, music, and theater plays. Today, the BBC World Service can be heard in English and 42 other languages.

Some children listened to the radio at school.

Chapter 6

The Golden Age and Today

The years from 1922 to 1952 are often called the Golden Age of Radio. Radios became very popular during this time. Most people did not have televisions until the late 1940s. Instead, they listened to the radio. They could hear comedies, dramas, music, and news. Children listened to adventure shows such as *The Lone Ranger*, *The Green Hornet*, and *Superman*.

Radios were important during World War II (1939–1945). They brought news about the war into people's homes.

During the Golden Age of Radio, many children listened to
adventure shows on the radio.

In 1942, the U.S. government formed the Voice of America. This program was sent to other countries. It told the news and American thoughts.

President Franklin D. Roosevelt understood the power of radio. He used the radio to talk to the American people. The radio brought his ideas into their homes. Roosevelt's broadcasts made people feel closer to him.

President Roosevelt's broadcasts were called "fireside chats."

Radios through the Years

Ward's Airline
1930

Packard Bell
1935

General Electric
1951

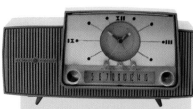

The radio remained popular even after most homes had a television. The radio gave people up-to-date news faster than the television. Radios were also cheaper to buy.

The radio is still important today. People around the world continue to tune in to hear broadcasts. There are now more than 2 billion radios and 33,000 radio stations across the globe.

Sony
1961

a radio from
1970s

a radio
today

Fast Facts

- In 1888, **Heinrich Hertz** showed that electromagnetic waves were real.

- **Radio waves** travel at the speed of light, 186,282 miles (299,792 kilometers) per second.

- **Guglielmo Marconi** was the first person to send a radio signal over a long distance.

- **KDKA** in Pittsburgh, Pennsylvania, was the first official radio station.

- There are more than **2 billion radios** and **33,000 radio stations** in the world today.

- In the 1990s, Trevor Baylis invented the **clockwork radio**. This radio does not need batteries. The user turns a handle to make the electricity that powers the radio. The clockwork radio is used in less developed countries where electricity is not always available.

Hands On:

Create Radio Waves

You can make your own radio waves and hear them over a radio.

What You Need
a small radio
a coin
a 9-volt battery

What You Do
1. Set the radio to receive AM broadcasts. Turn the radio dial until you find a place where you hear only static.
2. Hold the coin and battery near the antenna of the radio.
3. Tap the coin on the two terminals of the battery so that the coin connects the two terminals with each tap.
4. Listen to the radio as you tap the coin. Can you hear the crackling of your tapping through the radio speaker?

Together, the battery and coin act as a radio transmitter. They only transmit static, but if you know Morse code, you can tap out a real message over the radio with your battery and coin.

Glossary

broadcast (BRAWD-kast)—to send out news, music, weather, or other programs by radio; the programs that are sent out are called broadcasts.

frequency (FREE-kwuhn-see)—the number of complete electromagnetic waves in one second

invention (in-VEN-shuhn)—a new thing

microphone (MYE-kruh-fone)—a device used to change sound into electrical impulses

Morse code (MORSS KODE)—a system of dots and dashes used by the telegraph

radio wave (RAY-dee-oh WAYV)—a type of electromagnetic wave; electromagnetic waves are caused by electricity and magnetism.

transistor (tran-ZISS-tur)—a tiny electronic device that controls the flow of electrical current; transistors replaced the vacuum tubes in radios.

transmitter (transs-MIT-tur)—a device that sends out radio signals

Internet Sites

Do you want to find out more about the radio?
Let FactHound, our fact-finding hound dog, do the research for you.

Here's how:
1) Visit *http://www.facthound.com*
2) Type in the **Book ID** number:
   0736822178
3) Click on **FETCH IT**.

FactHound will fetch Internet sites picked by our editors just for you!

Read More

Birch, Beverley. *Guglielmo Marconi: Radio Pioneer.* Giants of Science. Woodbridge, Conn.: Blackbirch Press, 2001.

Mattern, Joanne. *The History of Radio.* Transportation and Communication. Berkeley Heights, N.J.: Enslow, 2002.

Mattern, Joanne. *The Radio: The World Tunes In.* Technology That Changed the World. New York: PowerKids Press, 2003.

Stille, Darlene R. *Radio.* Let's See. Minneapolis: Compass Point Books, 2002.

Index